MEDICAL DETECTING
DETECTING CANCER

by Matt Lilley

FOCUS READERS.
NAVIGATOR

WWW.FOCUSREADERS.COM

Copyright © 2024 by Focus Readers®, Lake Elmo, MN 55042. All rights reserved. No part of this book may be reproduced or utilized in any form or by any means without written permission from the publisher.

Focus Readers is distributed by North Star Editions:
sales@northstareditions.com | 888-417-0195

Produced for Focus Readers by Red Line Editorial.

Content Consultant: Scott Verbridge, PhD, Associate Professor of Biomedical Engineering and Mechanics, Virginia Tech

Photographs ©: Shutterstock Images, cover, 1, 8–9, 12–13, 17, 18–19, 21, 23, 26–27, 29; iStockphoto, 4–5, 7; American National Red Cross Photograph Collection/Library of Congress, 10; BSIP/Newscom, 15; Barnabas Honeczy/MTI/AP Images, 25

Library of Congress Cataloging-in-Publication Data
Names: Lilley, Matt, author.
Title: Detecting cancer / Matt Lilley.
Description: Lake Elmo, MN: Focus Readers, [2024] | Series: Medical
 detecting | Includes index. | Audience: Grades 4-6
Identifiers: LCCN 2023002509 (print) | LCCN 2023002510 (ebook) | ISBN
 9781637396230 (hardcover) | ISBN 9781637396803 (paperback) | ISBN
 9781637397893 (pdf) | ISBN 9781637397374 (ebook)
Subjects: LCSH: Cancer--Diagnosis--Juvenile literature.
Classification: LCC RC264.L55 2024 (print) | LCC RC264 (ebook) | DDC
 616.99/4075--dc23/eng/20230203
LC record available at https://lccn.loc.gov/2023002509
LC ebook record available at https://lccn.loc.gov/2023002510

Printed in the United States of America
Mankato, MN
082023

ABOUT THE AUTHOR

Matt Lilley has written 20 nonfiction children's books. He also has an MS in scientific and technical writing. The focus of his degree was on health writing for kids. He loves researching and writing about all sorts of topics. He lives in Minnesota with his family.

TABLE OF CONTENTS

CHAPTER 1
Searching for Skin Cancer 5

CHAPTER 2
Early Efforts 9

CHAPTER 3
Finding Physical Signs 13

CHAPTER 4
Examining Images 19

THAT'S AMAZING!
Detecting by Smell 24

CHAPTER 5
New Tools 27

Focus on Detecting Cancer • 30
Glossary • 31
To Learn More • 32
Index • 32

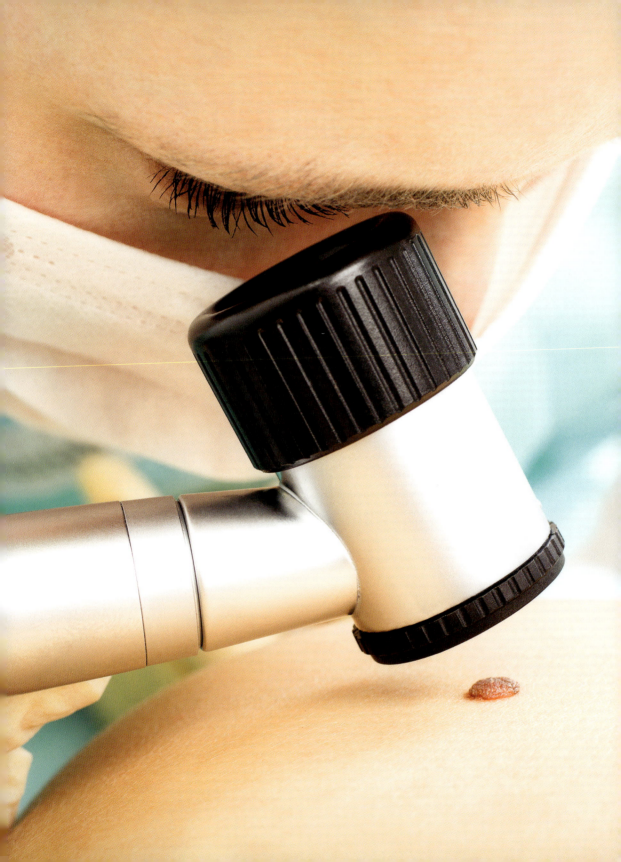

CHAPTER 1

SEARCHING FOR SKIN CANCER

A patient sits on an exam table. He takes off his shirt so his doctor can look at his skin. The doctor sees some freckles and moles. Most of them look **benign**. But one mole's border is uneven.

The doctor suspects this mole might be cancer. So, she decides to remove part

A physical exam is the best way to detect skin cancer. Doctors may use lights or magnifiers to check spots on patients' skin.

of it. First, she injects a painkiller next to the mole. Then, she makes a small cut.

The doctor sends the mole to a lab. A worker there looks at it under a microscope. He studies its **cells**. They are a type of skin cancer called melanoma.

The doctor needs to learn if the cancer has spread to other parts of the

SKIN CANCER SIGNS

Most people have some freckles or moles. Most of these spots are harmless. But some can be skin cancer. Cancerous spots often have bumpy edges. They may also change size, shape, or color. People can keep an eye out for these signs. They can have a doctor look at any unusual spots.

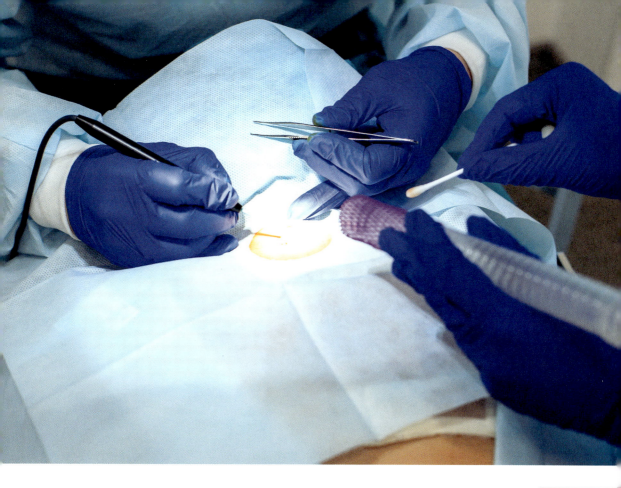

If moles or spots look unusual or dangerous, doctors do surgery to remove them.

patient's body. So, she orders a CT scan. If the cancer has spread, it could show up as spots in the scan. Fortunately, the patient's scan has no spots. His doctor has caught the cancer early.

CHAPTER 2

EARLY EFFORTS

For many years, cancer was very hard for doctors to treat. Doctors could see **tumors** on patients' bodies. But doctors weren't sure what caused them. And the patients were already seriously sick.

In the early 1800s, doctors began using microscopes. These tools helped doctors look at cells. Doctors learned

The microscope was an important invention for understanding the cells that cause cancer.

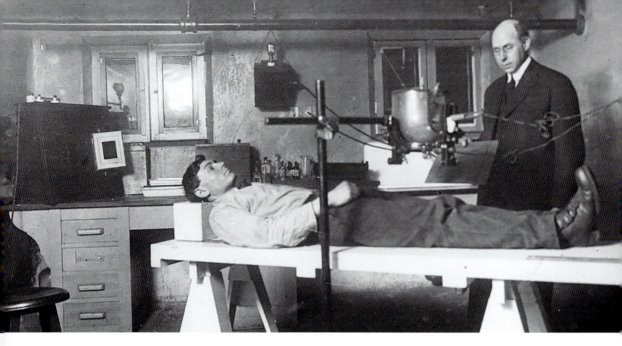

Early X-ray machines took longer to make images than today's machines do.

cancer cells were body cells that had **mutated**. This change made them grow and spread uncontrollably. Using microscopes, doctors could tell healthy cells and cancer cells apart. The cancer cells had irregular shapes and sizes.

But to look at cells, doctors had to take samples. Some cancers form in parts of the body that are hard to see or take pieces of, such as the brain or lungs.

In the 1890s, scientists discovered X-rays. Doctors began taking images that showed inside the body. They could see bones and other dense things, including some tumors. Since then, people have developed other imaging tools.

DANGEROUS RAYS

X-rays work by sending **radiation** through the body. Radiation can be dangerous. It can cause burns and cell damage. At first, no one knew this. Early X-rays exposed people to lots of radiation. Some patients got very sick. Some even died. Today, doctors work to protect patients from too much radiation.

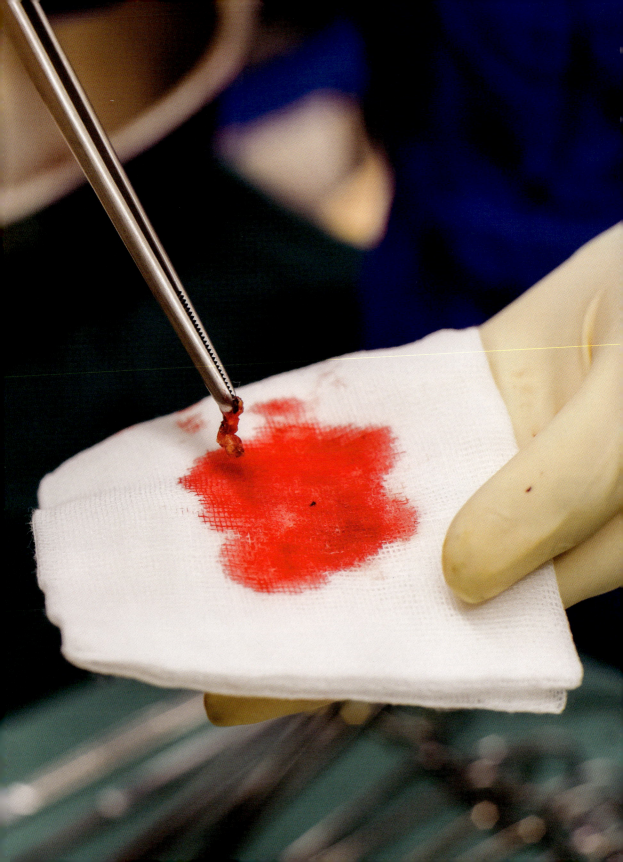

CHAPTER 3

FINDING PHYSICAL SIGNS

Physical signs are still one of the best ways to detect many types of cancer. People can check their bodies for unusual bumps or spots. If they find one, doctors can use a biopsy or other lab test to study it.

In a biopsy, a doctor uses a needle or knife to remove a small chunk of tissue

Depending on the type of cells being studied, biopsy results can take a few days or weeks.

from a person's body. This tissue is sent to a lab. Workers there look at its cells under a microscope. They can tell if the person has cancer. They can also learn what kind of cancer it is. This information helps doctors make plans for treatment. Doctors can tell how fast the cancer will

CANCER STAGES

Doctors use cancer stages to tell how much someone's cancer has grown and spread. This number system usually runs from 0 to 4. At stage 0, the cancer is in just one place. And it is still very small. By stage 2, the cancer has grown but not spread. Stage 4 is the most serious. At this stage, the cancer has reached other parts of the body.

grow. And they can see if it has started to spread to other parts of the body. Cancers that grow faster or are better at spreading are often more dangerous.

CANCER GRADES

Based on how cancer cells look under a microscope, doctors assign a grade. Cancers with higher grades tend to spread more quickly.

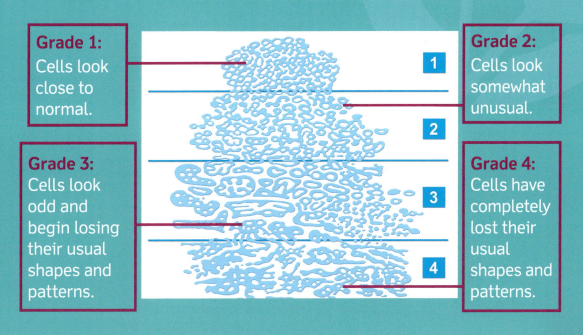

Grade 1: Cells look close to normal.

Grade 2: Cells look somewhat unusual.

Grade 3: Cells look odd and begin losing their usual shapes and patterns.

Grade 4: Cells have completely lost their usual shapes and patterns.

However, this method doesn't work for all cancers. Some cancers grow deep inside the body. And some are very small. Doctors use other types of lab tests to look for them. For example, cells from bladder cancer show up in a person's urine. So, doctors use urine tests to check for it. Leukemia is cancer of the blood. Blood tests help doctors detect it. The tests count the cells in a person's blood. Having high or low numbers of some cells can be a sign of cancer.

Cancer cells make certain chemicals. Blood tests can look for these **biomarkers**. Finding them can help doctors **diagnose** and treat cancer.

Lab workers use several types of machines to test blood for different chemicals.

Blood tests can also find cancer cells that have broken away from a tumor. These cells are a sign that a person's cancer might be spreading.

17

CHAPTER 4

EXAMINING IMAGES

Doctors use imaging to detect cancer as well. X-rays are still used for finding some types of cancer, such as bone cancer. But many newer technologies are also available. For example, a CT scan combines several X-rays. Each is taken from a different angle. A computer blends these X-rays together to create one

By studying scans, doctors can find tumors or other signs of cancer.

3D image. As a result, CT scans are much more detailed than standard X-rays. A CT scan can show a tumor's shape and the blood vessels going into it. Having this detail helps doctors track changes in the tumor. After a cancer treatment, doctors can do another CT scan to see if the tumor is shrinking.

GUIDED BIOPSIES

Imaging can also help doctors do biopsies. Sometimes, a tumor is deep inside the body. Doctors need to reach this place with a needle. They can do a CT scan while they insert the needle. The scan can show where the needle goes. That helps doctors avoid hitting other organs.

A scanner often has a round hole that the patient slides into.

Doctors also use MRIs. Like a CT scan, an MRI machine takes images from many angles. But an MRI uses strong magnets to make the images. The patient lies on a table that slides inside the machine. They must hold still and not wear anything metal. MRIs take better images of soft tissues and organs.

21

PET scans are used to check if cancer has spread throughout a person's body. Like MRIs, PET scanners are big machines. Patients lie on a table that slides inside. But before PET scans, patients are injected with sugar that contains a small amount of radiation. Cancer cells grow faster than other cells. So, they absorb more of this sugar. It makes them slightly radioactive. As a result, they get picked up by the scanner. A PET scan can find tumors that wouldn't show up in other images.

All of these images can be scanned into powerful computers. These computers look for patterns. They often use artificial

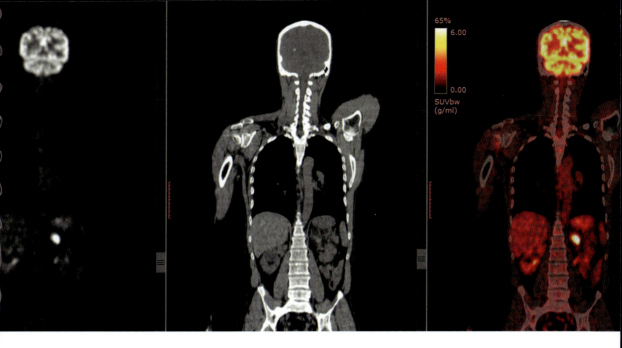

Cancer cells often show up in scans as bright spots.

intelligence (AI). AI allows machines to learn and make decisions on their own. For example, AI can check for signs of cancer. It can also help identify how big or fast-growing a tumor is. AI can check images much faster than humans can. And it can find things that people might miss.

THAT'S AMAZING!

DETECTING BY SMELL

Dogs have very sensitive noses. They can smell many things people cannot, including cancer. Dogs can find melanoma on a person's skin. They can smell bladder cancer in urine. They can even tell if someone has breast or lung cancer by sniffing the person's breath.

In the early 2000s, people started training dogs to sniff out cancer. Doctors collect samples from patients. With practice, dogs can tell healthy samples from cancerous ones. In fact, dogs are the best way to detect some cancers. For example, dogs correctly find prostate cancer 99 percent of the time.

Dogs are often trained to smell one type of cancer. But many can identify other kinds of

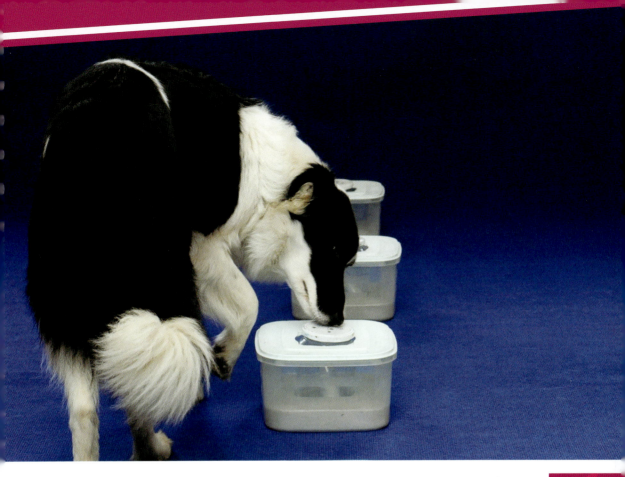

When smelling air people breathed out, dogs correctly identify cancer more than three-fourths of the time.

cancer, too. Scientists aren't sure how dogs do this. But they hope to make devices that can do something similar. Devices that detect odors already exist. AI could help these devices learn which odors mean cancer. As of 2023, this work is still in its very early stages.

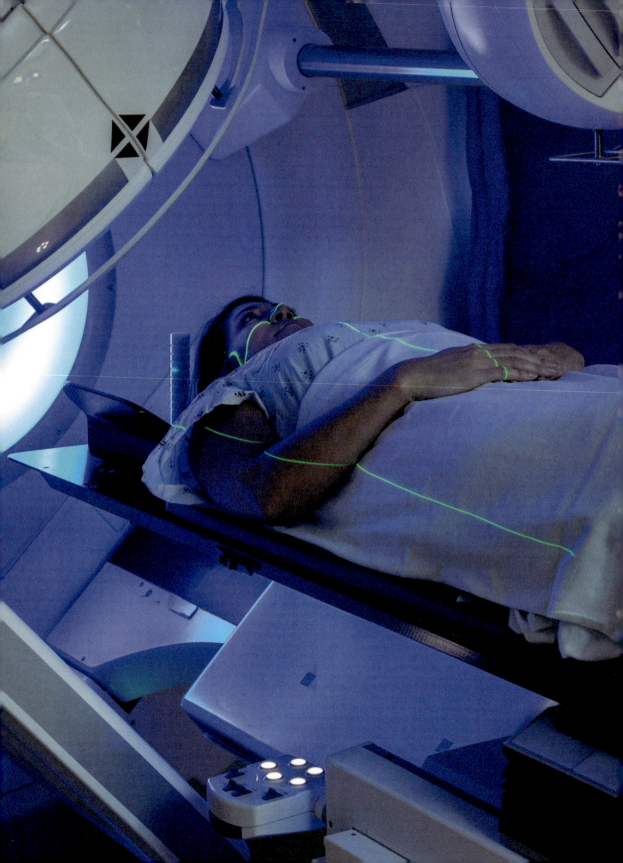

CHAPTER 5

NEW TOOLS

Cancer is most curable in the early stages. But many early cancers don't show up well on tests or scans. So, researchers focus on other ways to identify them.

For example, some cancers are linked to certain **genes**. Some behaviors and chemicals can make cancer more

Cancer treatments such as radiation tend not to work as well for later-stage cancers.

likely, too. Scientists can use computers to track these risk factors. They can find which people are most likely to develop cancer. Computers may also help scientists understand new risk factors. They could look for patterns among people who get sick.

Other research helps doctors find precancerous cells. These cells are beginning to have harmful changes. But they haven't yet become cancer. If doctors can remove these cells, patients may not develop cancer. Biomarkers can show if a person has precancerous cells. AI can help detect these biomarkers. It may also identify new ones. Both these methods

Smoking is one behavior that is known to cause cancer.

help doctors begin treatment sooner. That way, patients won't get as sick.

One day, doctors might even use smart toilets to check people's waste. The toilets would look for signs of sickness. For example, some **microbes** are associated with certain types of cancer. Finding these microbes in someone's waste could mean that person is sick.

29

FOCUS ON
DETECTING CANCER

Write your answers on a separate piece of paper.

1. Write a paragraph that describes the main ideas of Chapter 5.

2. Do you think computers with artificial intelligence might one day replace doctors? Why or why not?

3. Which type of imaging was invented first?

    A. PET scan
    B. MRI
    C. X-ray

4. What information could a CT scan include that an X-ray could not?

    A. A CT scan could show the inside of a person's body.
    B. A CT scan could show width, depth, and height.
    C. A CT scan could show the person's bones.

Answer key on page 32.

GLOSSARY

benign
Not dangerous.

biomarkers
Chemicals found in a person's blood or urine that are signs of changes or problems in the body.

cells
The smallest units of a living organism that can function and perform tasks.

diagnose
To identify an illness or disease.

genes
Tiny parts of cells that tell how to perform certain functions or cause the body to develop certain traits.

microbes
Tiny living things, such as bacteria.

mutated
Developed a new trait as a result of changes to genes.

radiation
Energy in the form of waves or particles.

tumors
Growths of abnormal tissue in the body.

TO LEARN MORE

BOOKS

Claybourne, Anna. *Cells.* London: Hachette Children's Group, 2022.

Kaminski, Leah. *The Science of Cancer.* Fremont, CA: Full Tilt Press, 2021.

Mooney, Carla. *Handling Cancer.* Minneapolis: Abdo Publishing, 2022.

NOTE TO EDUCATORS

Visit **www.focusreaders.com** to find lesson plans, activities, links, and other resources related to this title.

INDEX

artificial intelligence (AI), 22–23, 25, 28

biomarkers, 16, 28
biopsies, 13, 20
blood tests, 16–17

cancer grades, 15
cancer stages, 14, 27
computers, 19, 22, 28

CT scans, 7, 19–21

labs, 6, 13–14, 16

microscopes, 6, 9–10, 14–15
moles, 5–6
MRIs, 21–22

PET scans, 22

sniffer dogs, 24–25

tumors, 9, 11, 17, 20, 22–23

urine tests, 16

X-rays, 11, 19–20

Answer Key: **1.** Answers will vary; **2.** Answers will vary; **3.** C; **4.** B